DAUGHTERS OF BONE

DAUGHTERS OF BONE

Jessica Temple

MADVILLE
PUBLISHING

LAKE DALLAS, TEXAS

FIRST EDITION

Requests for permission to reprint or reuse material from this work should be sent to:

Permissions
Madville Publishing
PO Box 358
Lake Dallas, TX 75065

Publication Credits:

Many thanks to the editors of the following publications in which the poems in this collection have appeared, sometimes in previous versions.

"2508 Circle Drive": *decomP magazine*; "Anniversary": *The Red Clay Review*; "Barge & Blanket": *Juke Joint*; "Bearing": *Aesthetica Creative Writing Annual*, *Over 35, Under Pressure*, *A Year in Review: Out Loud HSV 2016*, and *Stone, River, Sky: An Anthology of Georgia Poems* from Negative Capability Press; "Black Rabbit": *The Red Clay Review*; "Cleansing": *Loose Change*; "Dépaysement": *Thema*; "Golden Shovel after Natasha Trethewey": *Juke Joint*; "Jawbone": *Peauxdunque Review*; "Littoral, Thalassic, Pelagic": *Loose Change*; "Mālama": *Canyon Voices*; "Mercy Breakfast": *Loose Change*; "My Grandmother Turns Eighty-Eight": *Canyon Voices*; "My Sister's Scar": *Peauxdunque Review*; "Seersucker": *Blast Furnace*; "Step/Mother": *Meniscus Literary Journal*; "Twisted": *Birmingham Arts Journal*; "Witch's Milk": *Agnes Scott College Writers' Festival Magazine*.

Many of these poems appeared in the chapbook, *Seamless and Other Legends*, published by Finishing Line Press.

Cover Art: Joshua Raymond, untitled watercolor
Cover Design: Jacqueline Davis
Author Photo: TC Caldwell, photographertc.com

ISBN: 978-1-948692-48-9 paper; 978-1-948692-49-6 ebook
Library of Congress Control Number: 2020941274

For my grandma, Bettye Kramer Cannizzo, who loved poetry and would have bought you a copy of this book, and to all those who fill in the gaps.

TABLE OF CONTENTS

One

Two

Three

Four

Five

DAUGHTERS OF BONE

One

"You can get there from here, though
there's no going home."

—*Natasha Trethewey*

Country Folk

We are country fried
and cornbread fed.
We are backwoods, down home,
nitty-gritty folks.
We work hard all day
to maybe work a little less
a little later on.
We live in Independence.
Reform. Reliance. Success.
Places that get so hot
your feet feel like they're burning
from both sides.
Triple digits? We shake it off.
Bills don't stop coming
just because it gets a little warm outside.
We use *lettuce* and *salad*
interchangeably, if at all,
and it's hard to be house-poor
in a double-wide.
But after the fur is done flying
and things settle back down,
we are the folks
who'll have what you need.
We'll be the last ones standing
when everything unravels.
We have the know-how
to do whatever it takes
and the firepower to back it up.
We can skin a buck,
grow near anything,
and build a fire
to burn all night.

Twins

for Vela

I. 1924

When you took ill at 7
scurvy was suspected.
Legend has it you got every orange
in Sevier County.

At first they must have been a treat,
something you'd only seen buried
under walnuts in Christmas stockings.
Rare, like ice cream or an airplane overhead.
You lay in bed and sucked them dry.

As time passed you grew tired
of sweet citrus: the stinging in your lips,
the strings between your teeth.
You asked for milk instead, warm in the pail.

When the fruit failed
and the milk began to curdle in the heat,
your sister placed pennies
on your eyelids.

It took three weeks for the doctor to come
and pronounce you dead.
He didn't think it was scurvy at all.
Said it was leukemia,
a word your parents had a hard time spelling.

They said there just weren't enough oranges.

II. 2011

When your eyesight began to go,
you relearned all the poems
you had memorized as a child.
Rote learning has its place, you said.

You worried that your great-grandson
might come sooner than predicted,
and when he was born early you weren't surprised.

You told your children
that you didn't mind going into the hospital,
but that you wouldn't be coming back out.

At your funeral,
we heard a story that
eighty-five years ago
you put pennies
over your dead brother's eyes.

Cad Dockery

Feel free to look him up. You won't find much:
b. 12 February 1900. d. April 1980.
last known residence: West Blocton, Bibb County, Alabama 35184.

What you won't find, at least without some digging:
that his brother reported him missing when he didn't show for their
    sister's funeral,
that a search warrant was granted after official letters went unanswered,
that investigators searched the house, but found nothing suspicious
until one cop stomped out a cigarette next to the back porch
and noticed a piece of a black plastic sticking out of the dirt.

He died at 80 of natural causes,
but rather than call the coroner,
his wife decided to bury him herself.
She was worried that authorities
would ask about the bullet wound
from when she'd had to shoot him in the leg
because he was casting a spell
to keep her from breathing.
But that was years ago. And he was so heavy
she couldn't move his body all at once
so she divided him into manageable portions,
parceled him out into trash bags
interred him a little at a time.

In the yard they uncovered a dozen buried bags
and every bone in Cad's body, save the toes.
Back in the lab they pieced him together, all 6-feet-3 of him,
his vertebrae calcified, fused so strong he could lift a Volkswagen.
And when they pulled the nylon socks out of his still-shiny shoes,
the last of his bones rattled inside.

Atnip Pushing Eighty

Mr. Atnip, pushing eighty and estranged
from all his sons—two co-owned a body shop,
the third, a florist nearby—
farmed five hundred acres on his own.
He hired help, a man named Hatchet,
when the ache in his bones
grew too great to work the fields alone.

Each month Atnip drove his old Ford to town,
endorsed his government check, passed it
to the teller for four crisp hundred dollar bills—
one for each week the money lasted.

One Saturday, Atnip's body was rolled
off his tailgate into a field near the airport.
Hatchet drove away with the truck
and two sharp hundreds, enough to buy
a weekend's worth of decent weed,
folded in his flannel shirt's front pocket.

Atnip left behind the trailer he'd lived in
long enough to shuffle around the floor's
weakest patches and a Smith and Wesson .38
so old and worn it could not be positively matched
to the bullets pulled from his chest.

Monday morning when Atnip's sons met
with investigators they asked only how soon
the five hundred acres could be divvied up.

Seersucker

*The word came into English from the Hindustani words "kheer aur shakkar,"
literally meaning "rice pudding and sugar," from the resemblance of its
smooth and rough stripes to the textures of milk and sugar.*

It seems so obvious now, knowing
the translation: the crumpled bumps
like grainy mounds of sugar, smooth
rivulets of cream creeping between.

Its slow interlacing, the threads wound
lazily onto two warp beams.
The stripes staying always on-grain
in that slow, slack-tension weave.

And wearing it, one feels slow, feels
the milkiness—the creamy thighs
sliding loose inside summer's shorts,
pale white skin hiding just under the cuff.

Sweat sneaks out, glitters under straw hats,
puckers sun-soaked skin like lemon
on the lips. Sweetness drips from tongues
in dewy voices, laden with white lies.

Heading North

I was twelve the summer my grandparents
took me to Michigan for a reunion—
three weeks away with no sick mother
or angry father, no little sisters
asking to play Polly Pocket
or walk to the store for push-pops.

We took our time, rolling past forests and fields,
crossing off states at their retirees' pace.
For once I had the whole luxurious backseat
to myself, reading or napping, spread across
all three sections of navy plush. We stopped mostly
at rest areas. I always signed the guest logs.

Somewhere along the way we found the best
pizza we'd ever had, bought roast beef
and apple cobbler for lunch the next day,
ate off a concrete picnic table at yet
another rest stop. The cobbler, even straight
out of the cooler, was perfect, its layers of dough
woven between lightly cinnamoned slices.

In Michigan, distant relatives. Great-aunts
and -uncles: all six of my grandfather's
siblings, all their wives and husbands, all
in one place for what turned out to be
the last time. Their children and grandchildren—
not all of them, but plenty—some I hadn't seen
in years, some never before or since.

I smiled for cameras, said *y'all* on request,
stopped asking for sweet tea. After a week
of official activities—after cookouts and card
tournaments, a slide show for old times' sake—
we three went with Uncle Bill and Aunt Charlotte
for a week on the lake at their Peppermint Cabin.

We took walks, watched birds, grilled burgers
and steaks at night, played cribbage and bridge.
Aunt Charlotte taught me how to shuffle sitting
on tall leather bar stools with a worn-out deck,
my fingers straining to copy the curve hers made.
From the backs of the cards, Joe Camel's smile
blurred past time after time as I perfected the arch.

One day we went to Mackinac Island,
where there are no cars. We rented bicycles,
ate warm fudge off a marble slab. As we ferried
back across, the lake spread like ocean out ahead.

Uncle Bill's false leg loomed that whole week.
Though I don't recall seeing it off him, I
couldn't help but glance down every so often
to catch the plastic shine above his sock. Stupid.
But that summer—for that summer I was just a kid.

Quilting

my mamaw learned it from her mother who learned it from hers
the stitches moving from one thin needle to the next—one visit
she brought her loom the aging wooden frame soon stretched its way
across our living room that whole week she fastened squares together

then layered batting and a cotton sheet her wrinkled fingers
went to work flying perfectly across the patchwork fabric
zipping stitches so tight so small and straight you'd never know
they were done by hand her needle inched up and down
up and down as many as six stitches at a time

my mother my sister and I helped too our little girl threads
too long and wobbling in the middle of the quilt we worked
underneath so we could reach the center the sun shining through
came from above covering us with its special kind of magic

The Visiting Writer

You think we're funny in heavy coats with no snow.
The women wear shoes, you say, you expected bare feet.
But that's only in summer, we tell you.

It's not survival of the fittest, you say, but survival
of the most adaptable, and works are always in progress.
Why, then, has your progress slowed, failed to change?

Don't be funny, you say,
although you, yourself, are funny
even if you don't intend it.

You ask us if we have tattoos, if we smoke a lot.
Strange questions from a man with sons our age,
and we're not sure how to answer.

Everyone has his own story, you say. Everyone
is broken. We are all damaged goods.
(This is what we have in common.)
So how do we undo the damage?
How do we adapt the shards?

2508 Circle Drive

cicadas on cedar
we wore as jewels
the smell of warm earth in the greenhouse   full of milk jugs
and circles
      always circles
           down ramps   up stairs
               through the kitchen   bedroom to bedroom

cutting roses from the garden
picking up crabapples
turning the crank on the big composter
      seeing more birds in the freezer than there really were

games of Casino
sawdust under the lathe in the shed
fresh-ground nutmeg
squirrels painted blue   bowling   French silk pie
half-door in the hallway
      and three
           protruding
               bricks

riding up the stairs
      in the white leather chair
           edged with brass tacks
the pass-through window in the kitchen
and the closet with the secret passage

      I still dream of finding other hidden doorways
           although I know it's the only one

Because It Is Growing Late in the Evening

and because she has a flight to catch the next morning,
she'll stop by for only a few minutes to say goodnight.

Dusk has already settled over the parking lot.
Crickets call to each other across the grassy lot between buildings.
The night is warm—early October in Alabama—
though the flowers' stamens have long since loosed their pollen.

Light trickles down from the partial moon and street lights overhead,
illuminating potholes in the unlevel asphalt.
Birds and squirrels that frequent the area in daylight are quiet now.
The oak and the poplar stretch their limbs overhead,
and the air is still and heavy, pinned by the heat of the day.

I lead my aunt through the gate, then the door.
We make our way down the bright tiled hall to Room 300.
Her mother's—my grandmother's—eyes light up to see us.

I straighten the things on the table, throw away trash as they talk,
step into the bathroom, giving them some privacy.
As I wash my hands, a silverfish slinks to the corner,
gliding as if carried by conveyor belt,
feet scurrying at a regimented pace beneath its black body,
oil-slick and smooth as glass.

If you knew you were seeing your mother for the last time,
would you say your goodbyes?
Or would you, too, stall?
Your butterflied stomach and corrugated heart,
not made for such open displays of emotion,
stopping you from stitching the bloodknot back together.

We leave after only a few minutes.
My aunt does not say goodbye.
Good night. I'll call you on Sunday, she says.

Blest be the tie that binds.
Blest be the tie that binds.

Whisper Work

Huntsville, Alabama

Seeing this place as my aunt must have seen it
fifty years ago as a teenager, new to town,
I understand her resentment, her hesitancy to visit.

She tells stories of a school separated not by race—
that was a given, then—but by locals versus "government."
The Joneses and Wallaces not mingling with Kradenskis and Cannizzos,
the names of immigrants trickling down from the North,
drawn southward by orders or the lure of lucrative engineering work.

The threatening phone calls they got in the summer of '67
that stopped her working with black children.

Her baptism out of religion, not one of fire, nor of water, but of wind—
the work of a whisper, violence in the voice.

Ghosts Floated Through My Childhood

My grandmother heard footsteps upstairs
just after Kennedy was shot. Why he stopped
at her house she never said. She and my grandpa
had both noticed the newspapers rustling
years before, at the moment her own grandmother
passed on.
        Papaw's story about the shortcut
through the cemetery, the white blob
coming slowly into view through the fog
and it waiting until he was just a few yards away
to moo.
        My mama's copy of *Thirteen Alabama Ghosts
and Jeffery*, edges worn, falling open to "The Specter
in the Maze." The trip down to Pickens County
to see the courthouse window for ourselves,
the black arrow pointing, unmistakably,
to the face etched there.
        My father talking to his father,
asking where he'd hidden the awl, or the auger,
or the ohmmeter, as if Papaw were playing a trick,
though he'd been dead for years.

Two

"O dear to me my birth-things—all moving things and the trees where I was born"

—*Walt Whitman*

Infestation

They first appeared on a blood-spotted handkerchief
soaking in your sink. Then, the weevils were everywhere:
the bedroom walls, the closet doors,
the shower curtain, the window sill.
We were sure it was a sign.

That first night, your neighbor,
swearing they would never cross baking soda,
poured a line of protection under her door,
but by morning she'd forgotten and wheeled right through
on her way to breakfast, leaving a powdery trail.
Pest control sprayed twice in seven days,
poured bleach down your drains.

Boll weevils, you called them, something familiar
to a Mississippi gal. The expert you mailed the black bodies to
said they were the rice variety instead. Either way,
they kept coming, antennae stretching from their faces
like tiny tridents, wings hidden beneath the gloss.

At first I pinched them up one by one between my nails,
squeezed until the shell snapped.
Later, I lifted them from surfaces with tape
and crunched them several at a time.

Finally I discovered the source:
the half-full bag of birdseed in your closet.
Held out from my body, I took it to the field,
and, spinning in circles,
slung the weevils out into arcs on the dried grass,
their legless, humpbacked offspring
still nestled in the seed.

Genotypical

Something compels the hair toward a certain color,
tells it to grow curly or straight, fine or thick.
Something picks the pigment of the skin,
the particular shade of olive, pink, brown.

Something forms the lips' pucker, juts the chin,
pulls the cheekbones back.
Something creates the contours of the nose,
shapes the eyes, tugs their corners

in one direction or another. Something tints the irises,
thickens eyebrows. Something determines the incisors'
shovel-shape, carves the tongue.
Something connects the lobes

or lets them dangle unattached.
Something establishes the slope of the forehead,
width of hips, capacity of chest cavity, the density of the bones.
Something stretches fingertips away from palms.

Trypophobia

1. Triggers

The lotus pod.
The honeycomb.
The underside of the tarantula's shed skeleton,
certain types of coral.

Aerated chocolate, soap bubbles,
a woodpecker's stash of acorns.
The blue-ringed octopus.

Sponges, condensation on a bottle.
Garlic cloves with the tops chopped off.
That species of frog whose babies hatch
out of its back.

A cantaloupe cut in half.
An image of cells dividing.
Rigatoni noodles.
A mud dauber's nest.

Swiss cheese, skin grafts,
the sourdough at Schlotzsky's,
a cluster of caterpillars.

A bowl of Cheerios.
Pebbles shaped into a man's face,
the abedus water bug
carrying his eggs,
a hair transplant.

A cut-away of a child's skull
before its milk teeth have fallen away.
Peach pits. A bundle of straws
seen from above. The seeds of a pomegranate.

2. The Dream

I stand in a towel looking into the bathroom mirror.
I notice a small round scab near my left shoulder,
just above where the towel tucks into itself,
and begin to scratch.

As the scab peels away, a narrow, yellowed grub,
tapered at both ends,
wriggles out.
I pick at another scab, and then another.
Each time something slithers out and drops.

Scratching away the last scabs,
I run screaming down the stairs, my hands
filling with the grubs—narrow ones
like soggy, bloated toothpicks,

others bright white and so fat they barely twitch.
They will not stop sliding
out of the lotus-shaped hollows
where my heart should be.

3. Research

Analysis uncovered similarities in the stimuli.
It has to do with luminance,
high-contrast energies,
wavelengths of light.

Some ancient, evolutionary part
recognizes the spectral characteristics,
associates the patterns with poisonous organisms.
We've been selected: Darwinian principles.

Everyone has trypophobic tendencies.

Api/Culture

Bees somehow know when their keeper is gone,
when someone new is obscured by the mesh.

Having teased out the nectar from sepals and pistils,
they will return sugar-drunk to their hives,
fidget their way in and out of the comb.

But they are agitated, aggravated
by this imposter. Smoke won't appease
these small riders of breezes.

All buzz and bustle, they go about their work,
feed their queen before seeing to their own needs.

They can tell one keeper from another,
but move their box just a few inches
and watch them go dizzy with confusion.

West Texas

Crop circles here
are not mysterious,
created by some starry stranger.
They are a way of life,
the only way to coax
living things from the dust.
Some grow in pairs,
a crop-encrusted
dusty reel-to-reel.
Some overlap
like records
stacked a little too loosely.
Dots on top of dots.
They brand the landscape
with half-moons
and slices of pie.
Sometimes the sun
sucks the droplets away
before they are absorbed.
Beyond Amarillo
the earth begins to turn
from coerced green
to its ordinary sandy hue.
One thin dirt trail
leads only to another.

Twisted

the day after

Plastic cups,
still in their dispenser,
rest in the rubble where a restaurant was.

The hospital saw 600 patients in the first 5 hours.
40 children arrived alone.
Don't come if you only have broken bones.

Red X's on cars,
just additional scars
added to those already torn through the skin of the city.

A mailbox,
the day's delivery still in place,
displays the address of the house that should be behind it.

A dog still chained to a tree uprooted
from another plot of land
must have surfed through the wind.

One man swears he was 30 feet above the ground,
riding in his iron bathtub,
Wizard of Oz style.

A cat found in a neighbor's apartment
hid under the wrong bed
since no walls are left between the two.

A student saw arms waving,
pulled a pregnant woman from under her house.
Then her child.
Then her mother.

My father saw a picture of a front door
with no house behind it.
Good thing you weren't home, he says.
The girl nods, says,
I was.

A young man threw his nearly naked body
over his neighbor. Not to be a hero,
but because he thought the world was ending
and he didn't want to be alone.

Cleansing

I know the man
in my dreams.
He shows up there
unexpectedly,
inappropriately.
In dreams, he eats
at my table,
leans far back
in my chair.
Stands too close
in my closet.

In real life,
he's never seen
my apartment.
But in dreams
he is haunting me,
like the word *loam*.

I have heard *loam*
five times this week,
maybe never before.

It started ordinarily,
in poems,
a gardening magazine.
But then, *loam*
on the radio.
Overheard
as the punchline
to an elevator joke.

To rid myself
I make it my own,
send *loam* back
underfoot. Tramp it
hard with my boot.
Pass over it.
Pass this
over to the man.

Beach in Winter

I am the gingerbread man,
the racetrack's rabbit.
I retreat as waves rush closer.
A sandpiper also scurries inland,
his tiny feet moving marvelously fast,
carrying him away faster than
my much larger ones.

I am the paparazzi
of seagulls.
No photos, he says, scooting away,
just out of camera's reach.
He pauses and looks back to see if I am gone.
I snap the shot; he prances off.
But it's all an act.
He enjoys the fame.

In the distance
the world disappears into the fog.
There are more shoed prints than bare.
I try to stay away from the edge,
to walk where the tide has been,
to search for half-buried treasures,
but the water draws me nearer
even as I resist.
This salty sand will stay in my shoes
long after I leave.

I choose no shells today.
Just a bit of coral
and one round, smooth rock
so perfect it must have tossed for years
in the ocean's depths.
As I walk back
I take it out of my pocket,
flip it over in my hand,
wonder if, to the rock,
that feels like home.

Poem from Within a Grave

The grass creeps up between my feet,
blades filleting me from the inside out.
Slowly roots take hold.
My hair grows longer through the dirt.
Later, the weeds come. Brittle stems
twist around my bones.
Grow green in my belly.

Diminishing

First it is a doubling. A repetition
of letters, of language. A joining
of like to like. It is a continuation,
a linking of poem to pomegranate.
One thing disappearing into another,
a sharing of bones and blood.
There is no separating of was from is.

Then there is a dividing. A fissure
of dark, of deep. An untethering
of same from same. It is an isolation,
a segregating of fire, of soot, of ash.
One thing drawing away from another,
an unraveling of skin from sinew.
There is no connecting of are with will be.

Bearing

My favorite part of baking is before:
the batter dripping from the paddle,
or the yeasty dome rising in the metal bowl.

*

Last week my aunt called to tell me
it's all right that I'm not pregnant.
I started to think maybe it's not.

*

Once, as warning, our grandmother told us about
her first husband—married because they had to.
Miscarried after a fall. Said she'd *prayed* for it.

*

One of those summers when heat
came early, a goat returned from the woods
with only one newborn. From the bulge

her belly had been, I knew that she
should've had two. I found the missing
by smell, just far enough in to stay shaded.

When I came back from shoveling,
it was already just a mound of fur,
wriggling with maggots inside.

*

My youngest sister asks me for recipes,
help with grammar. And when her doctor
said the pregnancy wasn't viable

she called me first. I could not
say to her *This is how
to lose your baby.*

*

Both my sisters now busy themselves
with the making of people. I've seen
the work of it, the pulling back

from the edge. One kept it covered
for months—hidden like shirt stays
under starched white trousers.

My nephews will be born
in Indian summer. One
will have dark skin, dark hair.

The other will be fair and
fearless. Both will grow tall.
They will not look like me.

Three

"You and I both know that the house is haunted.
You and I both know that the ghost is me."

—Shakey Graves

Family Name

In fourth grade we learned
that Leif Ericson was indeed the son of Erik.

And if, as I supposed,
the Taylors made clothing
and the Bakers bread,
and the Smiths shaped their gold and iron
over anvils throbbing
with heat and constant striking,
then what could my ancestors have done
but sell men?

Did my grandfather's grandfather's
grandfather man the trading block? Did he
tighten the chains, slapping
rusty metal against shining skin?

I pictured someone like my father,
equal in temperament but smaller in stature,
standing with crossed arms and pipe in hand
under a sign that reads

> *Mansell*
> *Purveyors of Fine Flesh*
> *Traders in Human Stock*

Cobbler

All we know for sure
is that he was a shoemaker:

He either died in battle
in World War I
or was run over
in the streets of Baltimore.

Stitching soles to welts,
vamps to toe caps.
Shaping the shank just right
before pressing in the name.

He made fettuccine,
enjoyed it with his favorite Orvieto,
or drank Barolo
with osso buco and roasted potatoes.

Attaching cuff, counter, quarter.
Firming up the backstay.
Perforating the leather
in patterns of dips and crests.

He loved Charlie Chaplin;
The Floorwalker was his favorite.
Or he didn't care too much for movies,
preferring to practice the violin.

Punching out eyelets
for later lace,
delicately hand-capped
with metal aglets.

He either came for the promise
of lower rent and softer leather
or because back home
was an accidental pregnancy and angry father.

Always moving seamlessly
from tongue to throat.

The Land Cruiser

On my dad's days off,
we'd load up in his old Land Cruiser,
dark as a fir tree
with a gleaming white hardtop.
We took backroads,
windows down, Daddy shifting
the flat black stick.
Mama sat shotgun,
my sister and I facing each other
from jumpseats in back.
Sometimes we'd take a friend,
ride two to a seatbelt.
We couldn't have been
more than 3 and 5, little enough
to still be in boosters,
but when we folded down those benches,
we rode our own private roller coaster.
We must have bumped over
every rutted muddy road,
splashed right across every creekbed
in the county. We'd strap in,
cinch the long belts tight across our laps,
and, giggling, skinny limbs
and ponytails flying, bounce along
with the pitch and jostle of the path.

Photograph of My Father as a Young Man

They say the first time is hard.
It gets easier after that.

Yours would have been a stranger,
a strange face, a stranger name.
A jungle far from home.

Triple digits—you shake it off,
sticky with sweat,
no time for cooling down.
The leaves slick with humidity.

You, skinny kid
in thick-rimmed glasses,
wild curls cropped close,
squint into the sun,
prop up your M14,
sit shirtless and
smiling for the camera.

Bài Thơ

My father's war came to me in bits and pieces—
the dark hand-carved coffee table,
the rainbowed bars near his shirt pocket,
the rice paper hat hanging in the hallway,
its crimped green ribbon,
its secret poem appearing like magic in the sun.

He spoke little of it, sticking instead to stories
of training exercises, long flights over the ocean,
the vital importance of a spare pair of socks.
Once, they caught a chicken running loose in the woods.
Once, he swam across a river—naked, or nearly so—
gripping the rope that would guide the others across.

I have his name patch on a seldom-used backpack
and his old foot locker with its worn-out lock by my bed.
We sprayed it red when I went to college,
but it's still olive drab on the inside.

Gotcha, He'd Say

My dad used to have a radar gun, a rounded relic
from his highway patrol days, metal crumpled
in places around the hard plastic dome, some
fallen spotlight grown dim. He kept it under
the driver's seat in the family van, plugged
into the cigarette lighter. When cars came
flying by, he'd flip it on for a second, watch
flickers of brake lights ahead, know without
seeing: first the look of panic, then the relief.

First Christmas

That first Christmas without her, I burned the chicken
we were supposed to have for lunch. My father,
just two weeks a widower, breaded the breasts,
left them frying on the stovetop, asked me
to keep an eye on it. But, distracted by presents,
I forgot. He flung the flaming pan off the porch,
burning the back of his hand. That year, we got
a Waffle House Christmas and a tile backsplash.

The year before I'd already found out that Santa
wasn't real. I was old enough to know better,
young enough to want to believe. On Christmas Eve,
my father woke me, late. Sneaking from the room
I shared with my sister, we walked down the dark hall
to the sunken den. He said presents were in his trunk.
I should make them look nice for my sisters.

Jawbone

There's a dead man living in my father's mouth.
Or maybe a dead woman, a child even. It's hard to say,
from such a small shard of collagen and calcium.

Grafted between two molars,
the cadaver's fragment spreads itself wide,
stretching to fuse into my father's jaw.

This bit of bone could have come from anyone:
a painter, a locksmith, a pleasant greengrocer,
a mute man whose own mouth never moved
except, with perfect teeth, to chew and chew.

Golden Shovel After Natasha Trethewey

"Your mother is dying," he yelled at
me in the cab of the red pickup, my
excuses no longer valid. Still, my mother's
illness did not seem real: a grave
mistake.

Once, when I was small, ants
covered my body. Water streamed
from the hose she held, covering me in
wet salvation, and
she stripped me bare.

I've never figured out
how to hold a memory like
a heart in my hands, its arteries
still pulsing. How to take a
thing, big as a monument, make it tiny:
mountain minimized to molehill.

With every rising
of the wide winter moon above
the water, I think of her,
her garden left untended,
an abandoning mid-plot.

Four

"This is the Hour of Lead–
Remembered, if outlived,
As Freezing persons, recollect the Snow–"

—*Emily Dickinson*

Mercy Breakfast

After my mother died
the Styrofoam cups lasted six years.
People we barely knew
offered casseroles and buckets
of chicken, paper plates,
cases of cokes.

Since my sisters
could not fill them out,
most clothes
came to me. We practiced
braiding her wig,
made it mat and tangle.

I don't know what happened
to her smooth prosthetic,
its flat side shining
like the layer that's skimmed off
after chicken boils.

By the time the pity food ran out,
I'd started starching shirt collars,
writing notes
on lunchbox napkins.
I already knew how to separate
the delicates,
how to slip an egg
over the edge of the pan
while it's still frying.

A Woman's Place

My husband will never understand
Why I have two stand mixers and one handheld
    in a galley kitchen
Why I refuse to pare down the four muffin tins:
    old and rusty, round microwavable, six-hole, red flexible
Why I keep a sifter from each grandmother—
    one with a crooked crank, one with a squeeze handle and two screens
Why I spend hours on pralines and divinity for holiday parties
    when I could just grab a bag of chips
Why I cried over the broken casserole dish
    that we'd only used twice
Why I use my mother's metal recipe box full of newspaper clippings and scraps of paper
    instead of looking online for directions from Paula Deen or Alton Brown
Why I think we need a butler's pantry
    complete with wine rack and an extra sink
Why I still make sausage balls every Christmas
    despite being a vegetarian
Why my baby sister calls me for advice
    on how to get a pie crust golden brown without it burning
Why I started out a string bean in slim-cut jeans,
    but turned out a little on the chunky side
Why I never measure salt

I tell him I don't understand it either
But my tongue knows the taste of not enough ginger
And my hands know when to stop kneading
And we're not quite there yet.

My Sister's Scar

The summer before our house was finished, our parents
rented a Ditch Witch to dig the water line themselves,
save some money. Kids that we were, my sisters and I
tossed a frisbee, ascended the trailer that had transported
the equipment, the bright orange rails and fenders an invitation.

Up and down we went, tracing sharp rainbows.
Jumped on and off like goats. Rebecca, at 3, kept up
until her little leg found the slit in the center
of the trailer. It slipped down easily, silently
as a single stand of spaghetti dangling through a slotted spoon.

But on the way back out her knee caught a rough spot
in the metal. She bled and cried,
but our parents were so far down the hill already.
Almost to the bottom, really. Instead I scooped her up,
carried her into the shimmering Airstream we had there.

She refused Bactine, wisely doubtful of its "no-sting" promise.
I washed the wound as best I could, bandaged it,
tied a tight bandana around. Somehow must have calmed her.
She was asleep by the time our parents got back.
They didn't want to wake her to examine the damage.

She still has the scar, which over the years has stretched
into a shiny earthworm of a thing, thick and banded,
and inched its way down her shin as if it remembers
the dirt, the ditch, the slot, the sting.
Everything that she's forgotten.

My Grandmother Turns Eighty-Eight

Wind pushes past us, hard and steady,
as we roll her down the gravel path
in a rented wheelchair,
her body hiding beneath a mass of yarn:
green sweater, gray toboggan,
patchworked granny-square blanket.
Bumping her across a bridge of two-by-fours,
we joke—my sisters, my aunt, and I—
of tipping her sideways
into the swampy shallows.
Our clicking hips and misaligned knees
carry us to the observation area's glass doors.

It takes time to spot across the field
what we have come to see:
seven white whooping cranes,
delicately balanced on thick black stilts.
We cannot hear their sounds,
which I imagine to be somewhere between
the screech owl's screech
and a phlegmy cough,
but we see their crispness
slide over the dull, brittle field
just above the stalks.

Funeral

for Laura

Right now, my best friend is flying to the coast
for her stepmother's funeral
three days after a sudden hospitalization.

Half-way through her second pregnancy,
she's left her son, who will be put to bed by his father
for the first time. She has the middle seat and hopes
she won't have to get up too often.

She has in her carry-on a skirt, two tops
and her mother's ashes, still sealed
in the box they were shipped in three weeks ago.

I knew both women, though mostly tangentially.
We were all at the wedding, and I'd met them each
once before. But over a friendship of fifteen years,
I've heard things. She's only going to help her half-sisters.

When my friend was young, the pseudo-mother
was busy raising her own daughters so sent her
not-daughter to boarding school. She never even met
her husband's only grandchild.

My friend's real mother didn't meet her grandson either,
prohibited by law from making the trip. She died a burden
to the state, twice-divorced, drug-addicted,
the Gabapentin or a lifetime of liquor finally catching up.

My friend has trouble coming up with even one
good memory of either woman. But tomorrow,
before the funeral, she will wade into the ocean
and dust the waves.

Step/Mother

Stepmothers were never as evil
as fairy stories would have us believe:
Poisoning apples and denying ball gowns.
Tempting fathers to abandon children.
Tricking youngsters into losing themselves in a wood.
Obliging their charges with all the housekeeping,
feeding them scraps meant for dogs or rubbish heaps
while fattening themselves on the best portions.

The *step* in *stepmother* is not a removal,
as in *a step away*.
Instead, it's from the German *stief*,
meaning grief,
as in bereavement, as in
the mother of bereaved children.

Stepmothers carry their children's grief
and their own as well—
that when those children loosed their birthcries
she was not there to quiet them.
She holds close that falseness, as in
not my mother when a mother is what is wanted.
See, it is not wickedness that leads stepmothers astray.
It is sadness.

Mother Holle

after the Brothers Grimm

Agéd mother of none, you waited
below the well in the nether regions
for a daughter of your own.

A drop of blood came first,
and then she fell from the sky,
a girl with flaxen braids and arms akimbo.
She noticed first your alarming teeth,
then the rest of you soon after.
She promised to keep your house
and fluff your feathered pillows.

When your golden girl grows lonesome
and returns to her rightful home,
no one will shake the down of your bed.
No one will wiggle the ripened apples from the trees.
No one will free the baker's bread from the ovens.

Next will come her wicked sister,
greedy for gold. In her laziness
she will leave the lumps under your covers.
You'll turn her black with sticky pitch
and send her home without her shuttle.

Alone again, you will mind your own house.
You will tend your own garden.
And when you set your own feathers flying
from your downy mattress,
we will call it snow.

Witch's Milk

My mother was born in the Mohave.
A few days later, her mama found small spots of blood
blooming in her diaper like brick dust settling.
The doctor explained that this sometimes happens
with babies born in deserts.
Having never seen it in her other daughters,
she thought this was the reason for the blood.
Something to do with the drier air.

Sixty years later, I read about witch's milk,
leaked from a baby boy's breasts,
and find that pseudomenses
results from the mother's hormones
withdrawing from her daughter's bloodstream,
just as hers must have dissipated from mine.
This dearth has nothing to do with the desert.

Inauguration Day

for my niece, Sharon Magdalena, on her first birthday

You came between snowstorms
under dull skies and bare branches
and the temperature in Callaway
stayed below freezing
for three days after you were born

We drove 740 miles over icy roads
to meet you, see your chubby pinked cheeks
and touch your tiny fat toes like candy
too sweet and too small to take seriously

You were named after the grandmother
you'll never know and Mary Magdalene—
saint of women—whose seven demons
whether sin or sickness, were drawn from her body

Today Callaway is 48 and rainy. You will celebrate
without understanding why, with cake and cousins
Meanwhile a man will place his hand
and take an oath. Another party taking over

While your family cheers for you
millions will cheer for him. Millions more
will mourn his ascent. Oblivious to this
you'll squeeze pink frosting between
your chubby fingers, giggle with the goosh of it
and lick banana cake off your knuckles

Today thousands of women will load
themselves onto busses, heading toward
the Capitol. As the sticky remnants are washed out
of your hair tonight, they will move steadily
converging from north, south, west

In the morning they will march

You will wobble, waddling
after dog or cat or brother

The women are mothers
They are aunts and grandmothers
sister, wife, daughter. They are
poets and teachers and doctors and
farmers and lawyers and bookstore owners
They are runners and gardeners
scrapbookers and smokers
dancers and kickboxers and bakers of cakes

They will march for themselves
for each other, for strangers
They will march for their bodies
their rights to their demons
their sins and sicknesses

They will carry their careful signs
and your future

Barge & Blanket

I am barge. I am blanket. This morning I was wrestling ring.
Before you were born I was cocoon, was chrysalis shell.
Then, I became bumper, burpcloth, bathmat.
Then, siren of police car and ambulance wailing together
with any threat of hurt or slight.
I was bottle before bowl, pacifier prior to plate.

Someday soon I will become launchpad. Become
starting line. Become rearview.
I'll be prologue, be remembrance.
But I will still be beacon in unfamiliar waters.
And barge when you need safe passage.
Be buoy when you find it difficult
                                        to float.

My Mother's Voice

When I hear my mother's voice on the cassette
it doesn't sound like I remember.
It's slower and deeper
with a strong Southern drawl
that's all but disappeared in my own
if I ever had it at all.

On the tape she talks with her mother
and her mother's mother—
three generations of women
reaching back even further,
telling stories of long-gone relatives
whose names I recognize
but whose voices I never heard.

This voice—her voice—
should be familiar to me
from thirteen years of
whispered shushes, bedtime stories,
"Too Ra Loo Ra Loo Ral"
sung soft and slow when I wouldn't sleep,
softball stand cheers,
and *hold still* reprimands mid-braid.

But somewhere along the way I've lost it,
supplanted her voice in my head
with my own. Her low legato lilt
replaced by my staccato soprano.
Her timbre hidden somewhere so deep
I've forgotten where to find it.

Jesus Year

At 40 I've reached a decade my mother never did.
My personal Jesus year come and gone already.
Every day now is a gift, a bonus, a chance to do the things
she might've done. I look at my aunts and try to find her face
at seventy, at fifty even: crinkled and sagging. Hair gone gray—
or white and soft as her mother's, who's 95 and just across town.

My friend says he would love to visit Scotland,
but how would he get there? His anxiety would never permit
a trans-Atlantic flight. And how will any of us get there, really?
Scotland or Seattle or C.E.O. or settled down with someone
and happy. Anything but lonely. Anywhere but here. Anywhere
but where we were that we never want to go back to.

I read that if you don't know what you want you can't make
good decisions. But sometimes all I want is to make good decisions
and leave the world better than I found it.

I'm 40 and too old to start over. I am who I am and I am not
who I thought I would be. I'm not crossing the ocean
but I've purchased a ticket. I can imagine the flight.
It's scary—terrifying, even—but I'm trying. And isn't that
all any of us can do.

Five

"… I have put my upper arm bones on
wrong, and never so much as today have I found myself
with all the road ahead of me, alone."

—*César Vallejo*

Dépaysement

The street outside my building looks more like a movie set
than any real place, with its storefront signs
and tables haphazardly scattered.

Even though I've been home for weeks, I can't shake the feeling
that the French call *dépaysement*, a sense of dislocation,
a word so un-Englishable.

Maybe it's the unsettledness of being a California widow, a wonder-wench
whose sweetheart lives elsewhere, prospecting
for nuggets in his own slow pan.

Today, a low Porsche I've never seen hunkers by the curb out front
like a wild thing ready to pounce, so sleek and slick and black
it almost disappears.

Alan and Anya

She looked to him for English-to-English translations.
Was mystified by turtles, watching their slimy tops bob in the water.
Did not understand about barbeque.
Enjoyed the view from the tower's observation deck.
Was amazed that his city had never seen modern warfare.
Tried fried okra.
Learned parts of the history that he'd not wanted her to see:
a crowded bus, a schoolhouse door.

Before she met him, Alabama was only a plastic magnet,
a trinket from another world.

From Sleep

This is a trick my mother taught me:
when thunder bumps you awake,
start counting mississippis.

Each second, she said, puts another mile
between you and the lightning's strike.

These days, when thunder comes
and I startle from sleep, I think
there's someone next to me, still sleeping,
maybe, or awakened also, back there
breathing heavily, eyes wide.

But nothing warm presses against my back.
Like some itching phantom limb,
only a cool hollow left to haunt me
between each flash and boom.

Americana, Brazil

That rebel flag holds no anger here—just a reminder
of where they came from, like their vinegar pies,
their Baptist churches. Senator Norris, one of thousands
of Confederate soldiers who went further south
to escape Reconstruction after all the damage
was done, settled here from Mount Pleasant.

A hundred miles inland from the sea and São Paulo,
his descendants remember their heritage fondly—
picnics with barbeque and fried chicken, an annual festival
with gray uniforms and dancing hoop-skirted girls,
the word *skillet* slipped in from a now-foreign tongue.

But for three generations they managed to keep
mostly to themselves—tending the land Dom Pedro offered,
cultivating their cotton and cane—those *Confederados*,
doling out their Southern drawls all over the jungle.

Black Rabbit

"…the parson of the village had a fancy for [Hildebrand's] wife, and had wished for a long while to spend a whole day happily with her."
                    —"Old Hildebrand" by Jacob and Wilhelm Grimm

Old Hildebrand, laurel wilds itself
waiting for your burlap,
its springy green oliving on the hill.
In the morning a sick child,
a sick husband, a sick wife,
or whoever else it may be
will lack restoration, and people
will lose faith in the words.

In the morning, Old Hildebrand,
you'll be a laughingstock.
In the morning your wife will repent
and will flapjack only for you.

But tonight the parson eats pancakes
and fiddles a fiddling tune.
His hotcakes steam on your table
and all of your chickens are dead.

Oh, Hildebrand, rise up now.
Rise up from your basket and sing.

Gregarious

If I were a songbird I would have
to hold the high notes, warble at just the right pitch.
Have to balance on the thinnest of appendages.

If I were a rabbit I would have to move my jaw
as if drawing tiny loops behind my lips,
get used to dashing away.

If I were a radish, I would be of the French Breakfast variety.
My piquant roots would grow away from my greens.
I would enjoy the moistness of the soil, germinate rapidly.

If I were you, I would talk more. Or talk less
but say more. I would listen, I would practice, I would pretend.
I would learn to fly and jump and push my stringy root deeper
into the earth.

Littoral, Thalassic, Pelagic

Pieces of sea drip from you:
the Pacific, the Gulf
of Mexico.
              The fishhook scars—
the L-slit entry on your palm
and puncture dot aligned
on the other side. And another,
hiding at the back of your head—
a slick, smooth slice on your scalp,
shining under hair, a dent, still discernible
after all these years—from falling
through the hatch to the cabin below.

The way you swear
that sailboat sank one night
with your whole sleeping family aboard
and resurfaced by morning,
your things drenched and salty.
You have no other explanation.

The way you casually mention
the mizzenmast and remember
to keep red on the right
when returning to port.

The way, beneath me, your body
turns to waves, your breath,
the roaring in my ears.

Mālama

You scratch your head in *pana poʻo* as if
you've forgotten banana trees in the backyard,
slippers beside the door, fresh coconut
sliced open by machete, your mother wading
through the house when a flood washed in one night—
the electrical current waving through the water,
shocking her ankles, her kneecaps—bringing you photos
and books to pat dry on the counter.

In the picture tucked into the family Bible,
you're a *haole* still in diapers,
kissing the little Hawaiian girl
on the beach at Kahanamoku,
your blond curls whispering
to her much darker ones.

Anniversary

Smell the strangeness of this southern city
Sunshine
Lost liquor
Sickening sea
Waking on a sticky Sunday
We walk to the end of the street
Watch the water
The bricks
The tapdancing boys
Held captive by different air
Optimistic air
But heavy
Laden with spirits
Of both kinds
We neglect the things
That brought us here
We listen instead
To calliope
And the glassharper
We are at once luxurious and wild
We have eaten and are full

A Study of Conjugation in Medias Res

And suddenly I wonder exactly how many times this had to happen
for both of us to be exactly here, exactly now.

How many generations of ancestors coupled at just the right time.
How many of them were happy, eager at the moment of conception.

How many consummating marriages. How many needed
more babies because the cards were stacked against them.

I wonder if any of the women were coerced, if the men were nervous,
telling themselves to *wait, wait* in some long-forgotten language.

All that sliding of skin, the gloss of sweat,
the small gasps escaping from the lips for centuries:

Our great-grandparents—in the Appalachian foothills in the First World War,
on a little farm in East Tennessee, somewhere near the Mississippi a few years later.

Then the grandparents, yours and mine, moving closer now—
Georgia, Alabama. And then my parents, in a trailer, I suppose

with a bunch of kittens in the blocks underneath,
red tractor and olive-lime Maverick parked out front.

And later, yours way out on the West Coast
smelling salt and sourdough. And then you.

You and me and right now.

About the Author

Jessica Temple earned her PhD in poetry from Georgia State University and teaches at Alabama A&M University. Her work has appeared in *Thema; Crab Orchard Review; Canyon Voices;* and *Stone, River, Sky: An Anthology of Georgia Poems*, among others. She is the author of the chapbook *Seamless and Other Legends* (Finishing Line Press, 2013). She attended the 2019 Sewanee Writers' Conference and was named Alabama State Poetry Society's 2019 Poet of the Year. Find out more at jessicatemple.com.

www.ingramcontent.com/pod-product-compliance
Lightning Source LLC
Chambersburg PA
CBHW031147090426
42738CB00008B/1257